# Rhythmic Gymnastics

by Julie Murray

Abdo Kids Jumbo is an Imprint of Abdo Kids
abdobooks.com

**abdobooks.com**

Published by Abdo Kids, a division of ABDO, P.O. Box 398166, Minneapolis, Minnesota 55439. Copyright © 2023 by Abdo Consulting Group, Inc. International copyrights reserved in all countries. No part of this book may be reproduced in any form without written permission from the publisher. Abdo Kids Jumbo™ is a trademark and logo of Abdo Kids.

Printed in the United States of America, North Mankato, Minnesota.

102022

012023

Photo Credits: Getty Images, Granger Collection, Shutterstock

Production Contributors: Teddy Borth, Jennie Forsberg, Grace Hansen
Design Contributors: Candice Keimig, Pakou Moua

Library of Congress Control Number: 2022937176

Publisher's Cataloging-in-Publication Data

Names: Murray, Julie, author.

Title: Rhythmic gymnastics / by Julie Murray

Description: Minneapolis, Minnesota : Abdo Kids, 2023 | Series: Artistic sports | Includes online resources and index.

Identifiers: ISBN 9781098264239 (lib. bdg.) | ISBN 9781098264796 (ebook) | ISBN 9781098265076 (Read-to-Me ebook)

Subjects: LCSH: Rhythmic gymnastics--Juvenile literature. | Gymnastics--Juvenile literature. | Aerobic dancing--Juvenile literature. | Sports--Juvenile literature. | Sports--History--Juvenile literature.

Classification: DDC 796.443--dc23

# Table of Contents

| | |
|---|---|
| Rhythmic Gymnastics . . . . . . . . . . 4 | More Facts . . . . . . . . . . . . . . . . . 22 |
| Props . . . . . . . . . . . . . . . . . . . . . . 10 | Glossary . . . . . . . . . . . . . . . . . . . 23 |
| What Gymnasts Wear . . . . . . . . 16 | Index . . . . . . . . . . . . . . . . . . . . . . 24 |
| Skills . . . . . . . . . . . . . . . . . . . . . . 20 | Abdo Kids Code . . . . . . . . . . . . . 24 |

## Rhythmic Gymnastics

Rhythmic gymnastics is a sport that combines gymnastics, ballet, and dance. Gymnasts perform a floor routine. It is set to music.

Gymnasts use **props** in their routines. They can perform solo or in groups.

Rhythmic gymnastics began in the 1800s in Europe. It was a way for gymnasts to **express** their emotions while exercising. It became a recognized sport in 1963. Today, it is an Olympic sport!

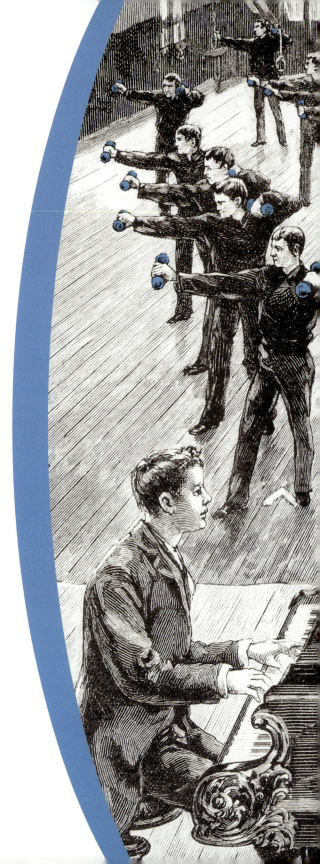

## Props

Rhythmic gymnastics has five events. Each event uses a different prop. The props are a ball, rope, ribbon, hoop, and clubs.

11

The **prop** needs to be in constant motion during the routine. A ball can be still only if it is balanced on the body.

13

**Props** are swung or twirled in a pattern. Gymnasts also toss and catch some of the props.

15

## What Gymnasts Wear

Gymnasts wear a leotard while performing. The leotard is decorated with crystals and beads. Matching outfits are worn in group performances.

Gymnasts also wear toe shoes to protect their feet. These shoes cover the toes while leaving the heel open. Toe shoes allow the gymnast to perform spins.

## Skills

Rhythmic gymnastics requires **flexibility** and strength. Good eye-hand coordination is also needed. Gymnasts often start training at an early age.

## More Facts

- Rhythmic gymnastics became an Olympic sport in 1984 for individuals. The group competition was added beginning with the 1996 Olympics.

- Rhythmic gymnastics is one of three sports in the Olympics that allow only women to compete. The others are synchronized swimming and softball.

- Gymnasts are scored on the difficulty and **execution** of the routine. Many factors go into each category for judging.

# Glossary

**execution** – the manner or quality of an action.

**express** – to make known or to show.

**flexibility** – the ability to easily bend without breaking.

**prop** – an item that is used in a performance or routine.

# Index

costume 16, 18

Europe 8

events 10

gymnast 4, 6, 14, 16, 18

history 8

music 4

physical health 20

props 6, 10, 12, 14

routine 4, 6, 12

shoes 18

Summer Olympics 8

team 6, 16

training 20

Visit **abdokids.com** to access crafts, games, videos, and more!

Use Abdo Kids code **ARK4239** or scan this QR code!